CCNP 300-101

IMPLEMENTING CISCO IP ROUTING

PRACTICE LABS AND SIMULATIONS

OSPF Evaluation Sim

You have been asked to evaluate an OSPF network and to answer questions a customer has about its operation. Note: You are not allowed to use the **show running-config** command.

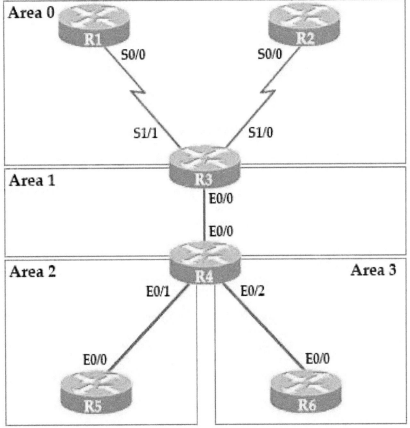

Although in this sim we are not allowed to use "show running-config" command but we post the configuration here so that you can understand more about the topology.

Some notices from above configuration:

+ The OSPF network type between R2 & R3 is non broadcast.

+ R3 and R4 is running virtual-link to connect Area 2 & 3 to Area 0

+ Area 2 is a NSSA area while Area 3 is a Totally Stubby area

R1
interface Loopback0
ip address 1.1.1.1 255.255.255.255
!
interface Serial0/0
ip address 192.168.13.1 255.255.255.0
ip ospf network non-broadcast
no shut
!
router ospf 1
network 192.168.13.0 0.0.0.255 area 0
network 1.1.1.1 0.0.0.0 area 0

R2
interface Loopback 0
ip address 2.2.2.2 255.255.255.255
!
interface S0/0
ip address 192.168.23.2 255.255.255.0
ip ospf network non-broadcast
no shut
!
router ospf 1
network 192.168.23.0 0.0.0.255 area 0
network 2.2.2.2 0.0.0.0 area 0
neighbor 192.168.23.3

R3
interface Loopback 0
ip address 3.3.3.3 255.255.255.255
!
interface Ethernet0/0
ip address 192.168.34.3 255.255.255.0
no shut
!
interface S1/0

```
ip address 192.168.23.3 255.255.255.0
ip ospf network non-broadcast
no shut
!
interface S1/1
ip address 192.168.13.3 255.255.255.0
ip ospf network non-broadcast
no shut
router ospf 1
network 192.168.13.0 0.0.0.255 area 0
network 192.168.23.0 0.0.0.255 area 0
network 192.168.34.0 0.0.0.255 area 1
network 3.3.3.3 0.0.0.0 area 0
area 1 virtual-link 4.4.4.4
neighbor 192.168.23.2
```

R4
```
interface Loopback 0
ip address 4.4.4.4 255.255.255.255
interface Ethernet0/0
ip address 192.168.34.4 255.255.255.0
no shut
!
interface Ethernet0/1
ip address 192.168.45.4 255.255.255.0
no shut
!
interface Ethernet0/2
ip address 192.168.46.4 255.255.255.0
no shut
!
router ospf 1
network 192.168.34.0 0.0.0.255 area 1
network 192.168.45.0 0.0.0.255 area 2
network 192.168.46.0 0.0.0.255 area 3
network 4.4.4.4 0.0.0.0 area 1
area 1 virtual-link 3.3.3.3
```

area 2 nssa
area 3 stub no-summary

R5
interface Loopback0
ip address 5.5.5.5 255.255.255.255
interface Loopback1
ip address 5.5.1.1 255.255.255.255
interface Loopback2
ip address 5.5.2.1 255.255.255.255
interface Loopback3
ip address 5.5.3.1 255.255.255.255
interface Loopback4
ip address 5.5.4.1 255.255.255.255
interface Ethernet0/0
ip address 192.168.45.5 255.255.255.0
no shut
!
router ospf 1
network 192.168.45.0 0.0.0.255 area 2
network 5.5.0.0 0.0.255.255 area 2
area 2 nssa

Question 1

How old is the Type 4 LSA from Router 3 for area 1 on the router R5?

A. 1858
B. 160
C. 600
D. 1569

Answer: A

Explanation

To check OSPF LSA we should use the "show ip ospf database" command on R5:

```
R5#show ip ospf database

            OSPF Router with ID (5.5.5.5) (Process ID 1)

            Router Link States (Area 2)

Link ID        ADV Router      Age     Seq#        Checksum Link count
4.4.4.4        4.4.4.4         415     0x80000004 0x006A66 1
5.5.5.5        5.5.5.5         424     0x80000004 0x004C59 2

            Net Link States (Area 2)

Link ID        ADV Router      Age     Seq#        Checksum
192.168.45.5   5.5.5.5         424     0x80000002 0x004B14

            Summary Net Link States (Area 2)

Link ID        ADV Router      Age     Seq#        Checksum
1.1.1.1        4.4.4.4         400     0x80000001 0x001FC1
2.2.2.2        4.4.4.4         483     0x80000001 0x00F0EB
3.3.3.3        4.4.4.4         1858    0x80000001 0x0040D8
4.1.4.4        4.4.4.4         1600    0x80000001 0x00080E
6.6.6.6        4.4.4.4         498     0x80000001 0x00B557
192.168.13.0   4.4.4.4         600     0x80000001 0x00026D
192.168.23.0   4.4.4.4         483     0x80000001 0x0093D1
192.168.34.0   4.4.4.4         501     0x80000001 0x009703
192.168.46.0   4.4.4.4         501     0x80000001 0x00137B
```

In this sim there is no LSA Type 4 because there is no ASBR so maybe this question wants to ask about LSA Type 3 (Summary Net Link States).

Note: LSA Type 4 is generated by ABR, not ASBR but without ASBR inside the network there are no LSA Type 4 generated.

R3 advertises LSA Type 1 to R4 then R4 converts it into Type 3 and sends to R5 (because R4 is the ABR) so we see the "Link ID" 3.3.3.3 of R3 is advertising by R4 (4.4.4.4). According to the "Age" column, this LSA was advertised 1858 seconds ago.

Question 2

Check the serial links connected to R3. Which statements are correct?

A. The neighbor command must be used on R1-R3 link to keep the adjacency up

B. The OSPF timer values of R2-R3 link are 30, 120, 120

C. The OSPF timer values of R1-R3 link should be 10,40,40

D. R3 must flood LSUs to all the routers on the network.

Answer: B

Explanation

Check the Serial1/0 interface of R3 which is connected to R2 with the "show ip ospf interface serial 1/0" command:

```
R3#show ip ospf interface serial 1/0
Serial1/0 is up, line protocol is up
  Internet Address 192.168.23.3/24, Area 0
  Process ID 1, Router ID 3.3.3.3, Network Type NON_BROADCAST, Cost: 64
  Transmit Delay is 1 sec, State DR, Priority 1
  Designated Router (ID) 3.3.3.3, Interface address 192.168.23.3
  Backup Designated router (ID) 2.2.2.2, Interface address 192.168.23.2
  Timer intervals configured, Hello 30, Dead 120, Wait 120, Retransmit 5
    oob-resync timeout 120
    Hello due in 00:00:03
  Supports Link-local Signaling (LLS)
  Index 2/2, flood queue length 0
  Next 0x0(0)/0x0(0)
  Last flood scan length is 1, maximum is 7
  Last flood scan time is 0 msec, maximum is 4 msec
  Neighbor Count is 1, Adjacent neighbor count is 1
    Adjacent with neighbor 2.2.2.2  (Backup Designated Router)
  Suppress hello for 0 neighbor(s)
```

There are two things we should notice from the output above:

+ The "network type" connection between R2-R3 is "NON_BROADCAST" (usually we have "BROADCAST"). OSPF neighbors are discovered using multicast Hello packets. In non broadcast environment, multicast (and broadcast) messages are not allowed so OSPF neighborship cannot be formed automatically. Therefore we have to establish OSPF neighborship manually by using "neighbor " command under OSPF process (OSPF will send unicast Hello message to this address). For example on R2 we have to use these commands:

> router ospf 1
> neighbor 192.168.23.3

And on R3:

> router ospf 1
> neighbor 192.168.23.2

+ For non broadcast environment the default Hello timer is 30 seconds; Dead timer (time to wait before declaring a neighbor dead) is 120 seconds and Wait timer (causes the interface to exit out of the wait period and select a DR on a broadcast network. This timer is always equal to the dead timer interval) is 120 seconds. In the output we also see the default timers for non broadcast network.

Question 3

OSPF uses the Shortest Path First (SPF) algorithm to find out the best paths. How many times was SPF algorithm executed on R4 for Area 1?

A. 2
B. 4
C. 9
D. 21
E. 25
F. 255

Answer: C

Explanation

We can check the number of executed SPF algorithm via the "show ip ospf" command on R4:

```
R4#show ip ospf
<output omitted>
Area 1
        Number of interfaces in this area is 2 (1 loopback)
        This area has transit capability: Virtual Link Endpoint
        Area has no authentication
        SPF algorithm last executed 00:01:51.544 ago
        SPF algorithm executed 9 times
        Area ranges are
        Number of LSA 12. Checksum Sum 0x053716
        Number of opaque link LSA 0. Checksum Sum 0x000000
        Number of DCbitless LSA 0
        Number of indication LSA 0
        Number of DoNotAge LSA 0
        Flood list length 0
<output omitted>
```

In the output above we can see SPF has been executed 9 times.

Question 4

Areas of Router 5 and 6 are not normal areas, check their routing tables and choose the best answer.

A. R5's Loopback and R6's Loopback are both present in R5's routing table
B. R5's Loopback and R6's Loopback are both present in R6's routing table
C. Only R5's loopback is present in R5's routing table
D. Only R6's loopback is present in R5's routing table
E. Only R5's loopback is present in R6's routing table

Answer: A

Explanation

Area 2 (of R5) is a Not-so-Stubby area (NSSA). You can check it by the "show ip ospf" command on R4 or R5 (in Area 2 section). For example, below is the output of "show ip ospf" command on R5:

```
R5#show ip ospf
<output omitted>
    Area 2
        Number of interfaces in this area is 6 (5 loopback)
        It is a NSSA area
        Area has no authentication
        SPF algorithm last executed 00:13:35.880 ago
        SPF algorithm executed 4 times
        Area ranges are
        Number of LSA 12. Checksum Sum 0x050250
        Number of opaque link LSA 0. Checksum Sum 0x000000
        Number of DCbitless LSA 0
        Number of indication LSA 0
        Number of DoNotAge LSA 0
        Flood list length 0
```

In general, NSSA is same as normal area except that it can generate LSA Type 7 (redistribute from another domain) so we can see both Loopback interfaces of R5 & R6 in the routing table of R5.

```
R5#show ip route

Gateway of last resort is not set

O IA 192.168.46.0/24 [110/2] via 192.168.45.4, 00:26:32, Ethernet0/0
        1.0.0.0/32 is subnetted, 1 subnets
O IA    1.1.1.1 [110/67] via 192.168.45.4, 00:26:32, Ethernet0/0
O IA 192.168.13.0/24 [110/66] via 192.168.45.4, 00:26:32, Ethernet0/0
        2.0.0.0/32 is subnetted, 1 subnets
O IA    2.2.2.2 [110/67] via 192.168.45.4, 00:26:32, Ethernet0/0
        3.0.0.0/32 is subnetted, 1 subnets
O IA    3.3.3.3 [110/3] via 192.168.45.4, 00:26:32, Ethernet0/0
C       192.168.45.0/24 is directly connected, Ethernet0/0
        4.0.0.0/32 is subnetted, 1 subnets
O IA    4.4.4.4 [110/2] via 192.168.45.4, 00:26:33, Ethernet0/0
        5.0.0.0/8 is subnetted, 5 subnets
C          5.5.5.5/32 is directly connected, Loopback0
C          5.5.1.0/24 is directly connected, Loopback1
L          5.5.1.1/32 is directly connected, Loopback1
C          5.5.2.0/24 is directly connected, Loopback2
L          5.5.2.1/32 is directly connected, Loopback2        R5's Loopbacks
C          5.5.3.0/24 is directly connected, Loopback3
L          5.5.3.1/32 is directly connected, Loopback3
C          5.5.4.0/24 is directly connected, Loopback4
L          5.5.4.1/32 is directly connected, Loopback4
        6.0.0.0/32 is subnetted, 1 subnets              R6's Loopback
O IA    6.6.6.6 [110/3] via 192.168.45.4, 00:26:33, Ethernet0/0
O IA 192.168.23.0/24 [110/66] via 192.168.45.4, 00:26:33, Ethernet0/0
O IA 192.168.34.0/24 [110/2] via 192.168.45.4, 00:26:33, Ethernet0/0
```

Note: NSSA does not receive a default route by default so you will not see a default route on R5.
Area 3 (of R6) is a Totally-Stubby area so R6 only has one default route to outside world. You can
check with the "show ip ospf" command on R4 and R6 (area 3 section):

```
R4#show ip ospf
<output omitted>
    Area 3
        Number of interfaces in this area is 1
        It is a stub area, no summary LSA in this area
           generates stub default route with cost 1
        Area has no authentication
        SPF algorithm last executed 00:21:58.840 ago
        SPF algorithm executed 5 times
        Area ranges are
        Number of LSA 4. Checksum Sum 0x02EA18
        Number of opaque link LSA 0. Checksum Sum 0x000000
        Number of DCbitless LSA 0
        Number of indication LSA 0
        Number of DoNotAge LSA 0
        Flood list length 0
```

```
R6#show ip ospf
<output omitted>
    Area 3
        Number of interfaces in this area is 2 (1 loopback)
        It is a stub area
        Area has no authentication
        SPF algorithm last executed 00:20:12.252 ago
        SPF algorithm executed 4 times
        Area ranges are
        Number of LSA 4. Checksum Sum 0x02EA18
        Number of opaque link LSA 0. Checksum Sum 0x000000
        Number of DCbitless LSA 0
        Number of indication LSA 0
        Number of DoNotAge LSA 0
        Flood list length 0
```

Notice that on R4 you will get more detail (shows "stub area, no summary LSA") than on R6 (only shows "stub area").

R6 is in a totally-stubby area so we will not see any R5's Loopback interfaces in R6 routing table:

```
R6#show ip route
Codes: C - connected, S - static, R - RIP, M - mobile, B - BGP
       D - EIGRP, EX - EIGRP external, O - OSPF, IA - OSPF inter area
       N1 - OSPF NSSA external type 1, N2 - OSPF NSSA external type 2
       E1 - OSPF external type 1, E2 - OSPF external type 2
       i - IS-IS, su - IS-IS summary, L1 - IS-IS level-1, L2 - IS-IS level-2
       ia - IS-IS inter area, * - candidate default, U - per-user static route
       o - ODR, P - periodic downloaded static route

Gateway of last resort is 192.168.46.4 to network 0.0.0.0

C    192.168.46.0/24 is directly connected, Ethernet0/0
     6.0.0.0/32 is subnetted, 1 subnets
C       6.6.6.6 is directly connected, Loopback0
O*IA 0.0.0.0/0 [110/2] via 192.168.46.4, 00:06:46, Ethernet0/0
```

Note: You can see a default (summary) route to the outside (O*IA 0.0.0.0/0 …)

EIGRP Evaluation Sim

You have been asked to evaluate how EIGRP is functioning in a network.

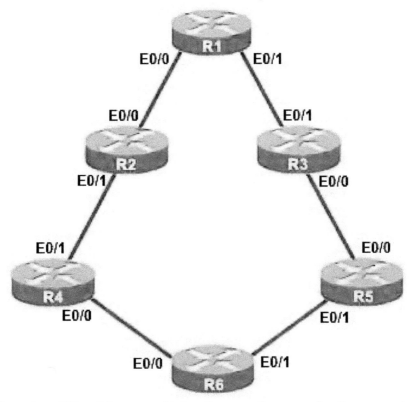

The configuration of R1 to R6 are posted below for your reference, useless lines are omitted:
Note: This sim uses IOS version 15 so "no auto-summary" is the default setting of EIGRP. You don't have to type it.

R1
interface Loopback0
ip address 150.1.1.1 255.255.255.255
!
interface Ethernet0/0
description Link to R2

```
ip address 192.168.12.1 255.255.255.0
ip bandwidth-percent eigrp 1 20
!
interface Ethernet0/1
description Link to R3
ip address 192.168.13.1 255.255.255.0
ip bandwidth-percent eigrp 1 20
delay 5773
!
router eigrp 1
network 192.168.12.0
network 192.168.13.0
net 150.1.1.1 0.0.0.0
variance 11
```

R2
```
interface Ethernet0/0
description Link to R1
ip address 192.168.12.2 255.255.255.0
!
interface Ethernet0/1
description Link to R4
ip address 192.168.24.2 255.255.255.0
ip authentication mode eigrp 1 md5
ip authentication key-chain eigrp 1 CISCO
!
router eigrp 1
network 192.168.12.0
network 192.168.24.0
!
key chain CISCO
key 1
key-string firstkey
key chain FIRSTKEY
key 1
key-string CISCO
key chain R3
```

key 1
key-string R3
key 2
key-string R1

R3
interface Ethernet0/0
description Link to R5
ip address 192.168.35.3 255.255.255.0
!
interface Ethernet0/1
description Link to R1
ip address 192.168.13.3 255.255.255.0
!
router eigrp 1
network 192.168.13.0
network 192.168.35.0

R4
interface Loopback0
ip address 150.1.4.4 255.255.255.255
!
interface Ethernet0/0
description Link to R6
ip address 192.168.46.4 255.255.255.0
!
interface Ethernet0/1
description Link to R2
ip address 192.168.24.4 255.255.255.0
ip authentication mode eigrp 1 md5
ip authentication key-chain eigrp 1 CISCO
!
router eigrp 1
network 192.168.46.0
network 192.168.24.0
network 150.1.4.4 0.0.0.0

```
!
key chain CISCO
key 1
key-string firstkey
```

R5

```
interface Ethernet0/0
description Link to R3
ip address 192.168.35.5 255.255.255.0
!
interface Ethernet0/1
description Link to R6
ip address 192.168.56.5 255.255.255.0
!
router eigrp 1
network 192.168.35.0
network 192.168.56.0
```

R6

```
interface Loopback0
ip address 150.1.6.6 255.255.255.255
!
interface Loopback1
ip address 172.16.6.6 255.255.255.255
!
interface Ethernet0/0
ip address 192.168.46.6 255.255.255.0
!
interface Ethernet0/1
ip address 192.168.56.6 255.255.255.0
!
router eigrp 1
distribute-list 1 out
network 150.1.6.6 0.0.0.0
network 172.16.6.6 0.0.0.0
network 192.168.46.0
network 192.168.56.0
```

!
access-list 1 permit 192.168.46.0
access-list 1 permit 192.168.56.0
access-list 1 permit 150.1.6.6
access-list 1 deny 172.16.6.6
access-list 2 permit 192.168.47.1
access-list 2 permit 192.168.13.1
access-list 2 permit 192.168.12.1
access-list 2 deny 150.1.1.1

Question 1

Traffic from R1 to R6' s Loopback address is load shared between R1-R2-R4-R6 and R1-R3-R5-R6 paths. What is the ratio of traffic over each path?

A. 1:1
B. 1:5
C. 6:8
D. 19:80

Answer: D

Explanation

First we need to get the IP address of R6's loopback address by "show ip interface brief" command on R6:

```
R6#show ip interface brief
Interface        IP-Address       OK? Method Status  Protocol
Ethernet0/0      192.168.46.6     YES manual up      up
Ethernet0/1      192.168.56.6     YES manual up      up
Loopback0        150.1.6.6        YES manual up      up
Loopback1        172.16.6.6       YES manual up      up
```

Now we learned the R6's loopback address is 150.1.6.6. To see the ratio of traffic that is load shared between paths, use the "show ip route 150.1.6.6" command on R1:

```
R1#show ip route 150.1.6.6
Routing entry for 150.1.6.6/32
  Known via "eigrp 1", distance 90, metric 461056, type internal
  Redistributing via eigrp 1
  Last update from 192.168.13.3 on Ethernet0/1, 00:29:07 ago
  Routing Descriptor Blocks:
    192.168.13.3, from 192.168.13.3, 00:29:07 ago, via Ethernet0/1
      Route metric is 1938688, traffic share count is 19
      Total delay is 65730 microseconds, minimum bandwidth is 10000 Kbit
      Reliability 255/255, minimum MTU 1500 bytes
      Loading 1/255, Hops 3
  * 192.168.12.2, from 192.168.12.2, 00:29:07 ago, via Ethernet0/0
      Route metric is 461056, traffic share count is 80
      Total delay is 8010 microseconds, minimum bandwidth is 10000 Kbit
      Reliability 255/255, minimum MTU 1500 bytes
      Loading 1/255, Hops 3
```

This means that after 19 packets are sent to 192.168.13.3, R1 will send 80 packets to 192.168.12.2 (ratio 19:80). This is unequal cost path Load balancing (configured with "variance" command).

Question 2

R6 is using a route filtering method. What type is it?

A. Distribute-list using an access-list
B. Distribute-list using a prefix-list
C. Distribute-list using a route-map
D. An access-list using a distance of 255

Answer: A

Explanation

Use the "show running-config" on R6 we will see a distribute-list applying under EIGRP:

```
R6#show running-config
<ouput omitted>
router eigrp 1
 distribute-list 1 out
 network 150.1.6.6 0.0.0.0
 network 172.16.6.6 0.0.0.0
 network 192.168.46.0
 network 192.168.56.0
 !
access-list 1 permit 192.168.46.0
access-list 1 permit 192.168.56.0
access-list 1 permit 150.1.6.6
access-list 1 deny 172.16.6.6
access-list 2 permit 192.168.47.1
access-list 2 permit 192.168.13.1
access-list 2 permit 192.168.12.1
access-list 2 deny 150.1.1.1
<ouput omitted>
```

With this distribute-list, only networks 192.168.46.0; 192.168.56.0 and 150.1.6.6 are advertised out by R6.

Question 3
The connection between R2 and R4 requires authentication. Which key chain is being used for this authentication?
A. CISCO
B. EIGRP
C. key
D. MD5

Answer: A
Explanation
Check on both R2 and R4:

```
R2#show running-config          R4#show running-config
<output omitted>                <output omitted>
key chain CISCO                 key chain CISCO
 key 1                           key 1
  key-string firstkey             key-string firstkey
key chain FIRSTKEY              !
 key 1                          <output omitted>
 key-string CISCO
key chain R3
 key 1
  key-string R3
 key 2
  key-string R1
 !
<output omitted>
```

To successfully authenticate between two EIGRP neighbors, the key number and key-string must match. The key chain name is only for local use. In this case we have key number "1" and key-string "CISCO" and they match so EIGRP neighbor relationship is formed.

Question 4
What is the advertised distance for the 192.168.46.0 network on R1?
A. 333056
B. 1938688
C. 1810944
D. 307456

Answer: A
Explanation

To check the advertised distance for a prefix we cannot use the "show ip route" command because it only shows the metric (also known as Feasible Distance). Therefore we have to use the "show ip eigrp topology" command:

```
R1#show ip eigrp topology
EIGRP-IPv4 Topology Table for AS(1)/ID(150.1.1.1)
Codes: P - Passive, A - Active, U - Update, Q - Query, R - Reply,
       r - reply Status, s - sia Status

P 192.168.24.0/24, 1 successors, FD is 307200
        via 192.168.12.2 (307200/281600), Ethernet0/0
P 192.168.35.0/24, 1 successors, FD is 793600
        via 192.168.13.3 (1785088/281600), Ethernet0/1
P 192.168.12.0/24, 1 successors, FD is 281600
        via Connected, Ethernet0/0
P 192.168.46.0/24, 1 successors, FD is 332800
        via 192.168.12.2 (1810944/333056), Ethernet0/0
P 150.1.1.1/32, 1 successors, FD is 128256
        via Connected, Loopback0
P 150.1.4.4/32, 1 successors, FD is 435200
        via 192.168.12.2 (435200/409600), Ethernet0/0
P 192.168.13.0/24, 1 successors, FD is 1759488
        via Connected, Ethernet0/1
P 150.1.6.6/32, 2 successors, FD is 460800
        via 192.168.12.2 (460800/435200), Ethernet0/0
        via 192.168.13.3 (1938688/435200), Ethernet0/1
P 192.168.56.0/24, 1 successors, FD is 358400
        via 192.168.12.2 (358400/332800), Ethernet0/0, serno 155
        via 192.168.13.3 (1810688/307200), Ethernet0/1
```

Update: Although the "show ip eigrp topology" does not work in the exam but the "show ip eigrp 1 topology" does work so please use this command instead and we will find out the advertised distance on R1.

There are two parameters in the brackets of 192.168.46.0/24 prefix: (1810944/333056). The first one "1810944" is the Feasible Distance (FD) and the second "333056" is the Advertised Distance (AD) of that route -> A is correct.

Just for your reference, this is the output of the "show ip route" command on R1:

```
R1#show ip route
Codes: C - connected, S - static, R - RIP, M - mobile, B - BGP
       D - EIGRP, EX - EIGRP external, O - OSPF, IA - OSPF inter area
       N1 - OSPF NSSA external type 1, N2 - OSPF NSSA external type 2
       E1 - OSPF external type 1, E2 - OSPF external type 2
       i - IS-IS, su - IS-IS summary, L1 - IS-IS level-1, L2 - IS-IS level-2
       ia - IS-IS inter area, * - candidate default, U - per-user static route
       o - ODR, P - periodic downloaded static route

Gateway of last resort is not set

D    192.168.46.0/24 [90/ 1810944] via 192.168.12.2, 00:10:01, Ethernet0/0
C    192.168.12.0/24 is directly connected, Ethernet0/0
L    192.168.12.1/32 is directly connected, Ethernet0/0
C    192.168.13.0/24 is directly connected, Ethernet0/1
L    192.168.13.1/32 is directly connected, Ethernet0/1
D    192.168.24.0/24 [90/1862144] via 192.168.12.2, 00:10:02, Ethernet0/0
D    192.168.56.0/24 [90/1810686] via 192.168.12.2, 00:10:01, Ethernet0/0
D    192.168.35.0/24 [90/1785088] via 192.168.13.3, 00:10:01, Ethernet0/1
     150.1.0.0/32 is subnetted, 3 subnets
D       150.1.6.6 [90/1938688] via 192.168.13.3, 00:10:03, Ethernet0/1
                  [90/461056] via 192.168.12.2, 00:10:03, Ethernet0/0
D       150.1.4.4 [90/158720] via 192.168.12.2, 00:10:04, Ethernet0/0
C       150.1.1.1 is directly connected, Loopback0
```

In the first line:

D 192.168.46.0/24 [90/ 1810944] via 192.168.12.2, 00:10:01, Ethernet0/0

The first parameter "90" is the EIGRP Administrative Distance. The second parameter "1810944" is the metric of the route 192.168.46.0/24. R1 will use this metric to advertise this route to other routers but the question asks about "the advertised distance for the 192.168.46.0 network on R1" so we cannot use this command to find out the answer.

Question 5
What percent of R1's interfaces bandwidth is EIGRP allowed to use?
A. 10
B. 20
C. 30
D. 40

Answer: B

Check with the "show running-config" command on R1:

```
R1#show running-config
<output omitted>
interface Ethernet0/0
  description Link to R2
  ip address 192.168.12.1 255.255.255.0
  ip bandwidth-percent eigrp 1 20
<output omitted>
```

In the "ip bandwitdh-percent eigrp 1 20" command, "1" is the EIGRP AS number while "20" is the percent of interface's bandwidth that EIGRP is allowed to use.

Note: By default, EIGRP uses up to 50% of the interface bandwidth. The bandwidth-percent value can be configured greater than 100%. It is useful when we set interface bandwidth lower than the real capacity of the link (for policy reasons, for example).

EIGRP OSPF Redistribution Sim

Question

Refer to the topology below.

+ The network requirements state that you must be able to ping and telnet from loopback 101 on R1 to the OPSF domain test address of 172.16.100.1.

+ All traffic must use the shortest path that provides the greatest bandwidth.

+ The redundant paths from the OSPF network to the EIGRP network must be available in case of a link failure.

+ No static or default routing is allowed in either network.

+ All IP addressing and basic routing have been completed.

+ You must complete the tasks and ensuring that the network requirements are met.

+ You may not remove or change any of the configuration commands currently on any of the routers. You may add new commands or change default values.

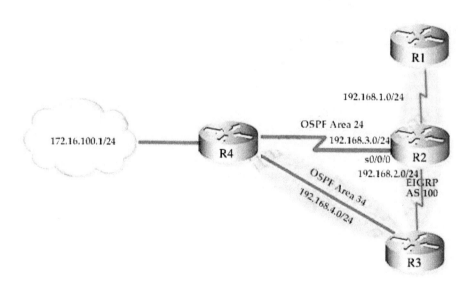

Answer and Explanation:

First we need to find out 5 parameters (Bandwidth, Delay, Reliability, Load, MTU) of the s0/0/0 interface (the interface of R2 connected to R4) for redistribution :

R2#show interface s0/0/0

Write down these 5 parameters, notice that we have to divide the Delay by 10 because the metric unit is in tens of microsecond. For example, we get Bandwidth=1544 Kbit, Delay=20000 us, Reliability=255, Load=1, MTU=1500 bytes then we would redistribute as follows:

R2#config terminal

R2(config)# router ospf 1

R2(config-router)# redistribute eigrp 100 metric-type 1 subnets

R2(config-router)#exit

R2(config-router)#router eigrp 100

R2(config-router)#redistribute ospf 1 metric 1544 2000 255 1 1500

(Notice: In fact, these parameters are just used for reference and we can use other parameters with no problem. Also, a candidate said that the simulator didn't accept the Bandwidth of 1544; in that case, we can use a lower value, like 128.

If the delay is 20000us then we need to divide it by 10, that is 20000 / 10 = 2000)

Note: "usec" here does not mean microsecond (which is 1/1000 milliseconds) but means millisecond. In short usec = msec. I don't know why they use the word "usec" here but just think it is "msec" (According to this link: http://www.cisco.com/en/US/tech/tk365/technologies_white_paper09186a0080094cb7.shtml#e igrpmetrics: "The delay as shown in the **show ip eigrp topology** or **show interface** commands is in microseconds")

For R3 we use the show interface fa0/0 to get 5 parameters too

R3#show interface fa0/0

For example we get Bandwidth=10000 Kbit, Delay=1000 us, Reliability=255, Load=1, MTU=1500 bytes

R3#config terminal

R3(config)#router ospf 1

R3(config-router)#redistribute eigrp 100 metric-type 1 subnets

R3(config)#exit

R3(config-router)#router eigrp 100

R3(config-router)#redistribute ospf 1 metric 10000 100 255 1 1500

Finally you should try to "show ip route" to see the 172.16.100.1 network (the network behind R4) in the routing table of R1 and make a ping from R1 to this network.

Note: If the link between R2 and R3 is FastEthernet link, we must put the command below under EIGRP process to make traffic from R1 to go through R3 (R1 -> R2 -> R3 -> R4), which is better than R1 -> R2 -> R4.

R2(config-router)# distance eigrp 90 105

This command sets the Administrative Distance of all EIGRP internal routes to 90 and all EIGRP external routes to 105, which is smaller than the Administrative Distance of OSPF (110) -> the link between R2 & R3 will be preferred to the serial link between R2 & R4.

A reader on our site has a closer explanation for the "distance eigrp 90 105" command so we quote it here for your reference:

The "distance" refers to the administrative distance of the routes provided by a given routing process. By default, internal (which means non-redistributed) EIGRP routes are given an administrative distance of 90 while external (redistributed from another routing process) EIGRP routes are given an administrative distance of 170. The default administrative distance of OSPF is 110. The administrative distance measures the "distance from the truth" and tells the router which routes are more trustworthy. Lower administrative distance = more trustworthy. For this reason, connected routes have an administrative distance of 0. They are the MOST TRUSTWORTHY, because they are physically connected to the router. When making a decision about which route to install in the routing table, the router looks at administrative distance first. The metric (or cost) is only considered if two routes have the same administrative distance.

In this case, R2 will learn about R4's loopback network from both R4 and R3. The route from R4 will be in OSPF (admin distance of 110) because R2 is also running OSPF while the route from R3 will be an external EIGRP route (administrative distance of 170 by default). Since the OSPF route has a lower administrative distance, it will get placed in R2's routing table and the R3-provided route will be ignored. This is not optimal, since the path through R3 is a faster, more reliable path. To fix this, we change the administrative distance of external EIGRP routes at R2 by using the "distance eigrp 90 105" command. This sets the administrative distance of internal EIGRP routes to the default of 90 and changes the administrative distance of external EIGRP routes to 105 (less than that of OSPF routes). Now, when R2 learns of the loopback network from R4 and R3, it will install the now lower administrative distance external EIGRP route from R3 and our traffic from R1 will take the faster path.

Note: Please check the OSPF process numbers first before typing these commands.
If you want to have a closer look at this sim and understand more about the "distance eigrp" command.

Policy Based Routing Sim

Company TUT has two links to the Internet. The company policy requires that web traffic must be forwarded only to Frame Relay link if available and other traffic can go through any links. No static or default routing is allowed.

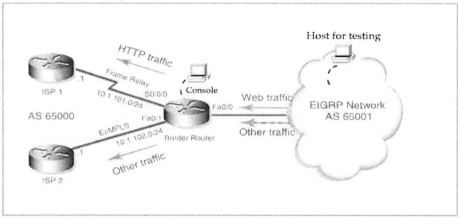

Notice: The answer and explanation below are from PeterPan and Helper.Please say thank to them!

All the HTTP traffic from the EIGRP Network should go through Frame Relay link if available and all the other traffic should go through either link.

The only router you are able to administrate is the Border Router, from the EIGRP Network you may only send HTTP traffic. As the other people mentioned, actually it is not a BGP lab. You are not able to execute the command "router bgp 65001"

1) Access list that catches the HTTP traffic:

BorderRouter(config)#access-list 101 permit tcp any any eq www

Note that the server was not directly connected to the Border Router. There were a lot of EIGRP routes on it. In the real exam you do not know the exact IP address of the server in the EIGRP network so we have to use the source as "any" to catch all the source addresses.

2) Route map that sets the next hop address to be ISP1 and permits the rest of the traffic:

BorderRouter(config)#route-map pbr permit 10

BorderRouter(config-route-map)#match ip address 101

BorderRouter(config-route-map)#set ip next-hop 10.1.101.1

BorderRouter(config-route-map)#exit

(Update: We don't need the last command **route-map pbr permit 20** to permit other traffic according to Cisco:

"If the packets do not meet any of the defined match criteria (that is, if the packets fall off the end of a route map), then those packets are routed through the normal destination-based routing process. If it is desired not to revert to normal forwarding and to drop the packets that do not match the specified criteria, then interface Null 0 should be specified as the last interface in the list by using the set clause."

Reference:

http://www.cisco.com/en/US/products/ps6599/products_white_paper09186a00800a4409.shtml)

3) Apply the route-map on the interface to the server in the EIGRP Network:

BorderRouter(config-route-map)#exit

BorderRouter(config)#int fa0/0

BorderRouter(config-if)#ip policy route-map pbr

BorderRouter(config-if)#exit

BorderRouter(config)#exit

4) There is a "Host for Testing", click on this host to open a box in which there is a button named "Generate HTTP traffic". Click on this button to generate some packets for HTTP traffic. Jump back to the BorderRouter and type the command "show route-map".

BorderRouter#show route-map

In the output you will see the line "Policy routing matches: 9 packets…". It means that the route-map we configured is working properly.

Question

TUT is a small company that has an existing enterprise network that is running IPv6 OSPFv3. However, R4's loopback address (FEC0:4:4) cannot be seen in R1. Identify and fix this fault, do not change the current area assignments. Your task is complete when R4's loopback address (FEC0:4:4) can be seen in the routing table of R1.

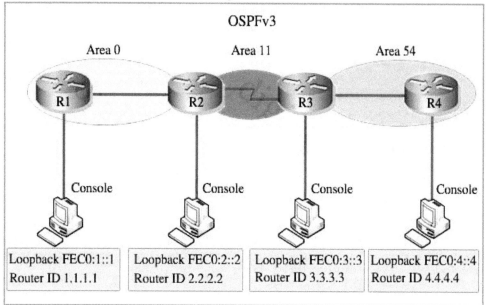

Special Note: To gain the maximum number of points you must remove all incorrect or unneeded configuration statements related to this issue.

Answer and Explanation:

To troubleshoot the problem, first issue the **show running-config** on all of 4 routers. Pay more attention to the outputs of routers R2 and R3

The output of the "show running-config" command of R2:

```
<output omitted>
!
ipv6 router ospf 1
router-id 2.2.2.2
log-adjacency-changes
!
<output omitted>
```

The output of the "show running-config" command of R3:

```
<output omitted>
!
ipv6 router ospf 1
router-id 3.3.3.3
log-adjacency-changes
area 54 virtual-link 4.4.4.4
!
<output omitted>
```

We knew that all areas in an Open Shortest Path First (OSPF) autonomous system must be physically connected to the backbone area (Area 0). In some cases, where this is not possible, we can use a virtual link to connect to the backbone through a non-backbone area. The area through which you configure the virtual link is known as a *transit area*. In this case, the area 11 will become the transit area. Therefore, routers R2 and R3 must be configured with the area *area-id* **virtual-link** *neighbor-router-id* command.

+ Configure virtual link on R2 (from the first output above, we learned that the OSPF process ID of R2 is 1):

R2>enable
R2#configure terminal
R2(config)#ipv6 router ospf 1
R2(config-rtr)#area 11 virtual-link 3.3.3.3
(Notice that we have to use neighbor router-id 3.3.3.3, not R2's router-id 2.2.2.2)

+ Configure virtual link on R3 (from the second output above, we learned that the OSPF process ID of R3 is 1 and we have to disable the wrong configuration of "area 54 virtual-link 4.4.4.4"):

R3>enable

R3#configure terminal

R3(config)#ipv6 router ospf 1

R3(config-rtr)#no area 54 virtual-link 4.4.4.4

R3(config-rtr)#area 11 virtual-link 2.2.2.2

We should check the configuration on R4:

R4>enable

R4#show running-config

You will see a wrongly configured virtual-link command. To get full mark we have to disable this command:

R4#configure terminal

R4(config)#ipv6 router ospf 1

R4(config-rtr)#no area 54 virtual-link 3.3.3.3

After finishing the configuration don't forget to ping between R1 and R4 to make sure they work well!

Now all the configuration was done. It is weird that we can't ping the IPv6 loopback interface of R4 (with the ping or ping ipv6 command) but we can check by using the command **show ipv6 route** on R1

The **copying running-config startup-config** command will not work but don't worry, just skip it.

Notice: If you issue the command "show running-config" on R1, you will see these two lines:

passive-interface default

no passive-interface fa0/0 (fa0/0 is the interface connecting with R2)

These two lines make all the interfaces of R1 become passive interfaces except interface fa0/0. They are correctly configured so don't try to disable them.

EIGRP Stub Sim

Question

TUT Corporation has just extended their business. R3 is the new router from which they can reach all Corporate subnets. In order to raise network stableness and lower the memory usage and broadband utilization to R3, TUT Corporation makes use of route summarization together with the EIGRP Stub Routing feature. Another network engineer is responsible for this solution. However, in the process of configuring EIGRP stub routing connectivity with the remote network devices off of R3 has been missing.

EIGRP

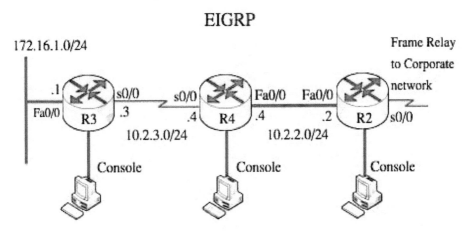

Presently TUT has configured EIGRP on all routers in the network R2, R3, and R4. Your duty is to find and solve the connectivity failure problem with the remote office router R3. You should then configure route summarization only to the distant office router R3 to complete the task after the problem has been solved.

The success of pings from R4 to the R3 LAN interface proves that the fault has been corrected and the R3 IP routing table only contains two 10.0.0.0 subnets.

Answer and Explanation:

First we have to figure out why R3 and R4 can not communicate with each other. Use the show **running-config** command on router R3

```
R3# show running-config
<output omitted>
!
router eigrp 123
network 10.0.0.0
network 172.16.0.0
no auto-summary
eigrp stub receive-only
!
<output omitted>
```

Notice that R3 is configured as a stub receive-only router. The **receive-only** keyword will restrict the router from sharing any of its routes with any other router in that EIGRP autonomous system. This keyword will also prevent any type of route from being sent.

Therefore we will remove this command and replace it with the **eigrp stub** command:

R3#configure terminal
R3(config)#router eigrp 123
R3(config-router)#no eigrp stub receive-only
R3(config-router)#eigrp stub
R3(config-router)#end

Now R3 will send updates containing its connected and summary routes to other routers. Notice that the **eigrp stub** command equals to the **eigrp stub connected summary** because the **connected** and **summary** options are enabled by default.

Next we will configure router R3 so that it has only 2 subnets of 10.0.0.0 network. Use the **show ip route** command on R3 to view its routing table

R3#show ip route

```
Router3# show ip route

10.0.0.0/8 is variably subnetted, 9 subnets, 2 masks

D        10.2.2.0/24 [90/30720] via 10.2.3.4, 00:00:06, Serial0/0

C        10.2.3.0/24 is directly connected, Serial0/1

D        10.2.4.0/24 [90/161280] via 10.2.3.4, 00:00:03, Serial0/0

D        10.2.5.0/24 [90/161280] via 10.2.3.4, 00:00:03, Serial0/0

D        10.2.6.0/24 [90/161280] via 10.2.3.4, 00:00:03, Serial0/0

D        10.2.7.0/24 [90/161280] via 10.2.3.4, 00:00:02, Serial0/0

D        10.2.8.0/24 [90/161280] via 10.2.3.4, 00:00:02, Serial0/0

D        10.2.9.0/24 [90/161280] via 10.2.3.4, 00:00:02, Serial0/0

       172.16.0.0/16 is variably subnetted, 2 subnets, 2 masks

D        172.16.0.0/16 is a summary, 02:04:27, Null0

C        172.16.1.0/24 is directly connected, FastEthernet0/0
```

Because we want the routing table of R3 only have 2 subnets so we have to summary sub-networks at the interface which is connected with R3, the s0/0 interface of R4.

There is one interesting thing about the output of the **show ip route** shown above: the **10.2.3.0/24**, which is a directly connected network of R3. We can't get rid of it in the routing table no matter what technique we use to summary the networks. Therefore, to make the routing table of R3 has only 2 subnets we have to summary other subnets into one subnet.

In the output if we don't see the summary line (like 10.0.0.0/8 is a summary...) then we should use the command ip summary-address eigrp 123 10.2.0.0 255.255.0.0 so that all the ping can work well.

In conclusion, we will use the **ip summary-address eigrp 123 10.2.0.0 255.255.0.0** at the interface s0/0 of R4 to summary.

R4>enable
R4#configure terminal
R4(config)#interface s0/0
R4(config-if)#ip summary-address eigrp 123 10.2.0.0 255.255.0.0

Now we jump back to R3 and use the **show ip route** command to verify the effect, the output is shown below:

```
Router3# show ip route

10.0.0.0/8 is variably subnetted, 2 subnets 2 masks

D      10.2.0.0/16 [90/2172416] via 10.2.3.4,00:00:11, Serial0/0

C      10.2.3.0/24 is directly connected, Serial0/0

172.16.0.0/24 is variably subnetted, 1 subnets

C      172.16.1.0/24 is directly connected, FastEthernet0/0
```

(But please notice that the ip addresses and the subnet masks in your real exam might be different so you might use different ones to solve this question)

But in your real exam, if you see the line "10.0.0.0/8 is a summary,....Null0" then you need to summary using the network 10.0.0.0/8 with the command "ip summary-address eigrp 123 10.0.0.0 255.0.0.0" . This configuration is less optimize than the first but it summaries into 2 subnets as the question requires (maybe you will not see this case, don't worry!).

The command "copy running-config startup-config" will not work so try using this command; just skip if it doesn't work.

OSPF Sim

Question

OSPF is configured on routers Amani and Lynaic. Amani's S0/0 interface and Lynaic's S0/1 interface are in Area 0. Lynaic's Loopback0 interface is in Area 2.

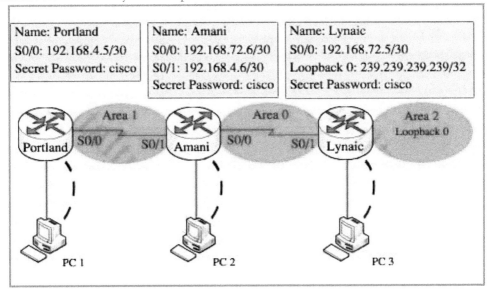

Name: Portland	Name: Amani	Name: Lynaic
S0/0: 192.168.4.5/30	S0/0: 192.168.72.6/30	S0/0: 192.168.72.5/30
Secret Password: cisco	S0/1: 192.168.4.6/30	Loopback 0: 239.239.239.239/32
	Secret Password: cisco	Secret Password: cisco

Your task is to configure the following:

Portland's S0/0 interface in Area 1

Amani's S0/1 interface in Area 1

Use the appropriate mask such that ONLY Portland's S0/0 and Amnani's S0/1 could be in Area 1.

Area 1 should not receive any external or inter-area routes (except the default route).

Answer and Explanation:

First, we configure Portland's S0/0 interface so that it belongs to Area 1. So, we have to find out which sub-network the IP address 192.168.4.5/30 (the IP of interface S0/0 of Portland) belongs to. This address belongs to a subnetwork which has:

Increment: 4 (/30 = 255.255.255.252 or 1111 1111.1111 1111.1111 1111.1100)

Network address: 192.168.4.4 (because 4 = 4 * 1 and 4 < 5)

Broadcast address: 192.168.4.7 (because 7 = 4 + 4 − 1) (It is not necessary to find out the broadcast address but we should know it)

The question requires that only Portland's S0/0 and Amani's S0/1 could be in Area 1, therefore we must use a wildcard of 0.0.0.3 (this wildcard is equivalent with a subnet mask of /30) so that there are only 2 IP addresses can participate in area 1 (they are 192.168.4.5 & 192.168.4.6). The full command we use here is **network 192.168.4.4 0.0.0.3 area 1**

The question also requires that "Area 1 should not receive any external or inter-area routes (except the default route)". Recall that if we don't want the router to receive external routes, we have to stop LSA Type 5. And if we don't want to receive inter-area routes, we have to stop LSA Type 3 and Type 4. **Therefore we have to configure area 1 as a totally stubby area.** For your information, here is the definition of a totally stubby area:

"**Totally stubb area** – This area does not accept summary LSAs from other areas (types 3 or 4) or external summary LSAs (Type 5). Types 3,4 and 5 LSAs are replaced by the Area Border Router(ABR) with a default router. Totally stubby areas protect internal routers by minimizing the routing table and summarizing everything outside the area with a default route." (CCNP BSCI Official Exam Certification Guide, Fourth Edition)

In conclusion, we have to configure area 1 as a totally stubby area. We do that by configuring Portland as stub and configuring Amani (ABR router) as a stub + "no-summary"suffix.

+ Configure Portland router as a stub:

Portland#configure terminal

Portland(config)#router ospf 1

Allow network 192.168.4.4/30 to join Area 1, notice that you have to convert subnet mask into wildcard mask:

Portland(config-router)#network 192.168.4.4 0.0.0.3 area 1

Configure Portland as a stub:

Portland(config-router)#area 1 stub

Portland(config-router)#end

Portland#copy running-config startup-config

+ Configure Amani router as a "totally stub":

Amani#configure terminal

Amani(config)#router ospf 1

Amani(config-router)#network 192.168.4.4 0.0.0.3 area 1

Make area 1 become a totally stubby area, notice that we can only use this command on ABR router:

Amani(config-router)#area 1 stub no-summary

Amani(config-router)#end

Amani#copy running-config startup-config

Note: Make sure to check the OSPF process ID before typing your configuration. Maybe it is not OSPF process 1 like the configuration above.

EIGRP – SHOW IP EIGRP TOPOLOGY ALL-LINKS

Here you will find answers to EIGRP Simlet question

Question

Refer to the exhibit. BigBids Incorporated is a worldwide auction provider. The network uses EIGRP as its routing protocol throughout the corporation. The network administrator does not understand the convergence of EIGRP. Using the output of the **show ip eigrp topology all-links** command, answer the administrator's questions.

```
Core1#show ip eigrp topology all-links
IP EIGRP Topology table for AS(65001) / ID (172.17.10.1)

Codes: P - Passive, A - Active, U - Update, Q - Query, R - Reply,
    r - reply Status, s - sia Status

P 172.17.3.128/25, 2 successors, FD is 30720, serno 9
    via 172.17.10.2 (30720/28160), FastEthernet0/1
    via 172.17.3.2 (30720/28160), FastEthernet0/3
P 10.140.0.0/24, 1 successors, FD is 156160, serno 16
    via 172.17.3.2 (156160/128256), FastEthernet0/3
    via 172.17.10.2 (157720/155160), FastEthernet0/1
P 172.17.10.0/24, 1 successors, FD is 28160, serno 1
    via Connected, FastEthernet0/1
P 172.17.0.0/30, 1 successors, FD is 20514560, serno 15
    via 172.17.1.1 (20514560/205122000), FastEthernet0/2
    via 172.17.10.2 (20516120/20513560), FastEthernet0/1
P 172.17.1.0/24, 1 successors, FD is 28160, serno 2
    via Connected, FastEthernet0/2
P 172.17.2.0/24, 1 successors, FD is 30720, serno 8
    via 172.17.10.2 (30720/28160), FastEthernet0/1
    via 172.17.3.2 (33280/30720), FastEthernet0/3
P 172.17.3.0/25, 1 successors, FD is 28160, serno 3
    via Connected, FastEthernet0/3
Core1#
```

Question 1

Which two networks does the Core1 device have feasible successors for? (Choose two)

A – 172.17.0.0/30
B – 172.17.1.0/24
C – 172.17.2.0/24
D – 172.17.3.0/25
E – 172.17.3.128/25
F – 10.140.0.0/24

Answer: A F

Explanation

To understand the output of the "show ip eigrp topology all-links command" command, let's analyze an entry (we choose the second entry because it is better for demonstration than the first one)

P 10.140.0.0/24, 1 successors, FD is 156160, serno 16
Feasible Distance→(156160/128256), FastEthernet0/3
      via 172.17.10.2 (157720/155160)←Advertised Distance

The first line tells us there is only **1 successor** for the path to 10.140.0.0/24 network but there are 2 lines below. So we can deduce that one line is used for successor and the other is used for another route to that network. Each of these two lines has 2 parameters: the first one ("156160" or "157720") is the Feasible Distance (FD) and the second ("128256" or "155160") is the Advertised Distance (AD) of that route.

The next thing we want to know is: if the route via 172.17.10.2 (the last line) would become the feasible successor for the 10.140.0.0/24 network. To figure out, we have to compare the Advertised Distance of that route with the Feasible Distance of the successor's route, if AD < FD then it will become the feasible successor. In this case, because AD (155160) < FD (156160) so it will become the feasible successor. Therefore we can conclude the network 10.140.0.0/24 has 1 feasible successor.

After understanding the output, let's have a look at the entire output:

```
Core1#show ip eigrp topology all-links
IP EIGRP Topology table for AS(65001) / ID (172.17.10.1)

Codes: P - Passive, A - Active, U - Update, Q - Query, R - Reply,
    r - reply Status, s - sia Status

P 172.17.3.128/25, 2 successors, FD is 30720, serno 9
    via 172.17.10.2 (30720/28160), FastEthernet0/1
    via 172.17.3.2 (30720/28160), FastEthernet0/3
P 10.140.0.0/24, 1 successors, FD is 156160, serno 16
    via 172.17.3.2 (156160/128256), FastEthernet0/3
    via 172.17.10.2 (157720/155160), FastEthernet0/1
P 172.17.10.0/24, 1 successors, FD is 28160, serno 1
    via Connected, FastEthernet0/1
P 172.17.0.0/30, 1 successors, FD is 20514560, serno 15
    via 172.17.1.1 (20514560/205122000), FastEthernet0/2
    via 172.17.10.2 (20516120/20513560), FastEthernet0/1
P 172.17.1.0/24, 1 successors, FD is 28160, serno 2
    via Connected, FastEthernet0/2
P 172.17.2.0/24, 1 successors, FD is 30720, serno 8
    via 172.17.10.2 (30720/28160), FastEthernet0/1
    via 172.17.3.2 (33280/30720), FastEthernet0/3
P 172.17.3.0/25, 1 successors, FD is 28160, serno 3
    via Connected, FastEthernet0/3
Core1#
```

Because the question asks about feasible successor so we just need to focus on entries which have more paths than the number of successor. In this case, we find 3 entries that are in blue boxes because they have only 1 successor but has 2 paths, so the last path can be the feasible successor. By comparing the value of AD (of that route) with the FD (of successor's route) we figure out there are 2 entries will have the feasible successor: the first and the second entry. The third entry has AD = FD (30720) so we eliminate it.

Question 2

Which three EIGRP routes will be installed for the 172.17.3.128/25 and 172.17.2.0/24 networks? (Choose three)

A – 172.17.3.128.25 [90/28160] via 172.17.1 2, 01:26:35, FastEthernet0/2

B – 172.17.3.128/25 [90/30720] via 172.17.3.2, 01:26:35, FastEthemet0/3

C – 172.17.3.128/25 [90/30720] via 172.17.10.2, 01:26:35, FastEthernet0/1

D – 172.17.2.0/24 [90/30720] via 172.17.10.2, 02:10:11, FastEthernet0/1

E – 172.17.2.0/24 [90/28160] via 172.17.10.2, 02:10:11, FastEthernet0/1

F – 172.17.2.0/24 [90/33280] via 172.17.3.2, 02:10:11, FastEthernet0/3

Answer: B C D

Explanation

First indicate the positions of these networks:

```
Core 1#show ip eigrp topology all-links
IP EIGRP Topology table for AS(65001) / ID (172.17.10.1)

Codes: P - Passive, A - Active, U - Update, Q - Query, R - Reply,
       r - reply Status, s - sia Status

P 172.17.3.128/25, 2 successors, FD is 30720, serno 9
    via 172.17.10.2 (30720/28160), FastEthernet0/1
    via 172.17.3.2 (30720/28160), FastEthernet0/3
P 10.140.0.0/24, 1 successors, FD is 156160, serno 16
    via 172.17.3.2 (156160/128256), FastEthernet0/3
    via 172.17.10.2 (157720/155160), FastEthernet0/1
P 172.17.10.0/24, 1 successors, FD is 28160, serno 1
    via Connected, FastEthernet0/1
P 172.17.0.0/30, 1 successors, FD is 20514560, serno 15
    via 172.17.1.1 (20514560/205122000), FastEthernet0/2
    via 172.17.10.2 (20516120/20513560), FastEthernet0/1
P 172.17.1.0/24, 1 successors, FD is 28160, serno 2
    via Connected, FastEthernet0/2
P 172.17.2.0/24, 1 successors, FD is 30720, serno 8
    via 172.17.10.2 (30720/28160), FastEthernet0/1
    via 172.17.3.2 (33280/30720), FastEthernet0/3
P 172.17.3.0/25, 1 successors, FD is 28160, serno 3
    via Connected, FastEthernet0/3
Core 1#
```

Network 172.17.3.128/25 has 2 successors, therefore the two paths below are both successors.

Network 172.17.2.0/24 has only 1 successor, therefore the path lies right under it is the successor.

Question 3

Which three networks is the router at 172.17.10.2 directly connected to? (Choose three)

A – 172.17.0.0/30
B – 172.17.1.0/24
C – 172.17.2.0/24
D – 172.17.3.0/25
E – 172.17.3.128/25
F – 172.17.10.0/24

Answer: C E F

Explanation

```
Core1#show ip eigrp topology all-links
IP EIGRP Topology table for AS(65001) / ID (172 17 10 1)

Codes: P - Passive, A - Active, U - Update, Q - Query, R - Reply,
    r - reply Status, s - sia Status

P 172.17.3 128/25, 2 successors, FD is 30720, serno 9
    via 172 17 10 2 (30720/28160), FastEthernet0/1
    via 172.17 3 2 (30720/28160), FastEthernet0/3
P 10.140.0 0/24, 1 successors, FD is 156160, serno 16
    via 172 17 3 2 (156160/128256), FastEthernet0/3
    via 172 17 10 2 (157720/155160), FastEthernet0/1
P 172.17 10 0/24, 1 successors, FD is 28160, serno 1
    via Connected, FastEthernet0/1
P 172.17.0 0/30, 1 successors, FD is 20514560, semo 15
    via 172 17 1 1 (20514560/205122000), FastEthernet0/2
    via 172 17 10 2 (20516120/20513560), FastEthernet0/1
P 172.17.1 0/24, 1 successors, FD is 28160, serno 2
    via Connected, FastEthernet0/2
P 172.17 2 0/24, 1 successors, FD is 30720, serno 8
    via 172 17 10 2 (30720/28160), FastEthernet0/1
    via 172.17 3 2 (33280/30720), FastEthernet0/3
P 172.17 3.0/25, 1 successors, FD is 28160, serno 3
    via Connected, FastEthernet0/3
Core1#
```

First, we should notice about the entry in the orange box, it shows that the network 172.17.10.0/24 is directly connected with this router and has a FD of 28160. So we can guess the networks that directly connected with router at 172.17.10.2 will be shown with an AD of 28160. From that, we find out 3 networks which are directly connected to the router at 172.17.10.2 (they are green underlined). The network 172.17.10.0/24 is surely directly connected to the router at 172.17.10.2 (in fact it is the network that links the router at 172.17.10.2 with Core1 router).

www.ingramcontent.com/pod-product-compliance
Lightning Source LLC
LaVergne TN
LVHW052316060326
832902LV00021B/3935